Contents

For the Instructor

Why Teach Literature?

The ability to communicate distinguishes humans from other forms of animal life. This ability to communicate has enabled us to not only meet our most basic needs but also to share our most eloquent thoughts and lofty dreams. When these thoughts and impressions are shared in the form of written language, they become literature. For the reader, literature is one form of self-expression that can take us beyond the limitations of our own situation and carry us to other times and places. Without moving from our comfortable chair, we can experience distant places and travel into the past and future. Without risking bodily injury, we can vicariously take part in breath-taking adventures. We can try on different personalities, experiment with new ideas, and feel a wide range of emotions. Through the pages of a book, we can take part in a life far grander and more diversified than the one we actually live.

Literature should be an integral part of the reading program for all students. Literature gives students an opportunity to apply the skills that are developed through basal readers and workbooks. It entertains while building the ability to imagine and developing intellectual skills. It gives readers the opportunity to think about feelings, morals, and values and helps them define the relationships between other people. Literature exploration takes students beyond skill building and lets them grown intellectually, emotionally, and in aesthetic appreciation.

Helping children appreciate literature and instilling a love of reading is perhaps one of the most precious gifts a teacher can give his or her students. We are glad that you chose *Inside Stories* to help you with this task. We are sure that these guides will provide many hours of reading enjoyment and material for thought provoking.

About this Book

This book is one in a series entitled *Inside Stories*. Each book contains ten literature guides. The books have been grouped according to grade levels and include a variety of literature types. Each edition is designed to introduce students to several different genres of literature as well as a variety of skills. These texts were developed in the Bartholomew Consolidated School Corporation for use with fourth through eighth grade students. The intent is to give teachers an easyto-use vehicle to introduce students to literature appreciation and analysis.

These study guides were designed to be used in a situation in which the teacher directs discussion groups consisting of a small group of students. They can also be used with cluster grouping or with an entire class with aides or volunteers serving as discussion leaders.

Each book in this series consists of the following materials:

1. Instructors' Notes

This page includes suggested grade levels, a brief biography of the author, a synopsis of the book, suggestions for themes, literary objectives (including exploration of the plot, character development, themes, and writing techniques), and a list of companion titles. Instructors will find this page helpful in planning the general direction and specific goals they wish to accomplish for a book.

2. Reading Assignments

These reproducible pages break the novel into manageable sections and provide vocabulary words and questions for each reading assignment. For some books, the list of vocabulary words is quite extensive, so instructors may wish to select only some of the suggested vocabulary words. Questions are designed to test students' comprehension of the material but also to draw them into higher-level thinking. Instructors may ask students to write the answers to the questions before discussing them as a group. These questions are not the single-answer or fill-in-the-blank variety. Therefore, students should be encouraged to provide complete, thoughtful answers. An answer page or section with specific answers is not given, because this would tend to indicate that there is one "right" answer. Instead, as answers are discussed, instructors should ask for explanations and justifications rather than settling for a single correct answer. Many of the questions ask for interpretations or evaluations. It can be expected, therefore, that students will have a variety of answers and should be given the opportunity to discuss and compare their ideas.

3. Conclusion and Summary

This reproducible page looks at the entire book and draws all elements into focus. These questions require higher-level thinking skills of analysis, synthesis, and evaluation and divergent interpretations. They are intended to give students an opportunity to draw comparisons and conclusions and to apply ideas to their own lives. Students should be asked to review each question carefully and give answers that reflect their understanding of the entire story. They should use examples and quotations to support their answers wherever appropriate.

4. Activities

This reproducible page presents several enrichment activities to expand students' understanding of the book. These activities are a combination of research or individual interpretation of the concepts presented in the book and a finished product that is the vehicle for displaying or communicating those ideas. Students should be instructed to select those activities that enable them to use their creative abilities and present their ideas about the book. Instructors may wish to work with individual students to create other activities that will be showcases for their ideas about the book or provide opportunities for doing in-depth research on individually-selected topics.

Behavioral Objectives

As a result of using the materials in this book, students may be expected to accomplish the following:

1. Students will develop an awareness and appreciation of a wide variety of good literature.
2. Students will develop and make use of the higher-level thinking skills of analysis, synthesis, and evaluation.
3. Students will develop oral and written communication skills.
4. Students will increase their written and oral vocabulary.
5. Students will understand and be able to recognize the elements of a story (setting, problem, climax, and ending).
6. Students will understand, be able to recognize, and be able to create their own samples of literary techniques and strategies.
7. Students will be able to identify themes and apply concepts presented in the books to their own lives.
8. Students will be able to make judgments concerning morals and values as presented in the books.
9. Students will be able to analyze characters, their traits, motives, and feelings and compare characters to themselves.

Instructor's Role

The instructor plays an important role in bringing literary works to life in the classroom. It is important that students sense that the teacher values reading and literature. The literature exploration that begins in the classroom setting should spill over into all areas of students' lives. To do this, teachers need to help students discover the relationship between the situations and concepts presented in each book and their own lives. It is important, therefore, that the teacher establish an atmosphere where students feel free to express their opinions. Students should be encouraged to elaborate on their answers, justify their evaluations, and interject their own feelings. In addition to the questions that are provided, teachers should ask probing questions that will guide students to define their thoughts and feelings. There should also be less emphasis on objectives testing and more emphasis on subjective forms of evaluation. This would include evaluating students' learning via written assignments, essays, reports, activities, and discussions.

Across Five Aprils
Irene Hunt

Suggested Reading Level
Grades 7-8

Biography
Irene Hunt was born in 1907 in Illinois. Ms. Hunt is a former school teacher, and she uses her understanding of youngsters as she tries to capture special moments and feelings for her readers. *Across Five Aprils* won the Newbery Honor Award in 1965, and her book, *Up The Road Slowly,* won the Newbery Award in 1967. Another well-known book by this author is *No Promises in the Wind*.

Synopsis
Historical Fiction
Jethro Creighton is a young man growing up in southern Illinois in the 1860's. The book follows this young man and his family during the years of the Civil War. The family is torn between loyalties. The book is historically researched and based on the many stories told to the author by her grandfather.

Themes
1. Loyalty
2. Impact of the past on the present
3. Revolution and political conflict
4. Family conflict
5. Price of freedom

Literary Objectives
1. Analyze the character development, theme, plot, and setting
2. Determine cause and effect relationships
3. Identify the author's purpose and style

Companion Titles
1. *Johnny Tremain* – Esther Forbes (impact of past on present, revolution and political conflict, price of freedom, coping with conflict)
2. *The Pushcart War* – Jean Merrill (revolution and political conflict, cause and effect)
3. *Freedom Train* – Dorothy Sterling (price of freedom, Civil War)

Across Five Aprils
Chapter 1

Vocabulary

furrow	secession	monotonous	typhoid	apathy
imminence	melancholy	inclination		acrid

1. The author gives the reader a great deal of information about the setting in the first paragraph. List the facts given.

2. Why was Shadrach a hero to Jethro?

3. How was the use of a dialect effective? Give examples.

4. Ellen Creighton felt that destiny had marked Jethro. What did this mean?

5. Who was president, and what issues did he face in 1861?

6. What history had the Creighton family experienced with war?

7. How did the community feel toward Matt Creighton?

8. Who was Jethro's favorite in the family and why? How did the community feel about Bill? Why?

9. Describe the special relationship between John and Bill.

10. How did Jethro see war in this first chapter? How did his feelings about war differ from his mother's?

11. What were the most strenuous tensions the family felt?

Across Five Aprils
Chapters 2-3

Vocabulary

puny   providence   oratory   abolitionists   secession
arrogant   tariff   tumult   pious   fiasco

1. What problems faced the Creightons with the war news from Wilse?

2. Why might England have helped the South in the war effort?

3. What issues led to the beginning of the Civil War?

4. What bothered Bill so much about the war issue?

5. What was bothering Jethro?

6. Describe the two types of slavery Bill thought about.

7. What caused the fight between Bill and John?

8. What final advice did Bill give to Jethro before he left?

9. How was the Creighton family changing?

Across Five Aprils

Chapter 4

Vocabulary

tyrannical   mimicry   skepticism   dispel   scornful
distortion

1. Why were Fort Henry and Fort Donelson important to the war?

2. What news about the war did Tom send in his letter?

3. How was the traditional housing policy changed when Shadrach came to teach?

4. What did Shadrach mean when he said, "Thou too, Brutus"? From where did this famous line come?

5. What did Shadrach mean by, "The dreams of men in my generation are . . .insignificant"?

6. How were the rivers important to the war effort?

7. Why was Jethro rebuked by Shadrach?

8. What were some of the things that Shadrach said to Jethro that made an impression on him during their visit?

9. How did Shadrach and Jethro feel about Bill fighting for the South?

Across Five Aprils
Chapter 5

Vocabulary

stoic   forte   dissipated   astute   sinister   resonance
terrain   precariously   appalled

1. Why was Ellen so ill?

2. How was Jethro's role changing in his family?

3. How did the farmers get word about the war and battles?

4. What concerned Jethro as he traveled by the Burdow's place?

5. Describe the town of Newton.

6. What problems was the free state of Illinois having?

7. What ridicule did Jethro encounter because Bill was fighting for the South?

8. How was Milton's school experience different from Jethro's?

9. What did Milton do that helped Jethro most?

10. What did Jethro face on the return trip from Newton?

11. Why do you feel Dave Burdow helped Jethro?

Across Five Aprils
Chapters 6-7

Vocabulary

prophecy   tenacious   ominous   ruffians   gullibility
integrity   malice

1. What created the drastic change in Jethro's role as a family member?

2. How was the relationship changing between Jethro and Jenny?

3. By reading the paragraph about praise from Matt, what would seem to have been the pioneer philosophy?

4. Why did Jethro react the way he did to Jenny's love letter?

5. Jethro thought fondly of the word "April." What ideas did the word represent for him? Why?

6. Matt said, "This war is a beast with long claws." This is an example of a metaphor. What did he mean? Create your own metaphor for war.

7. What had happened to the various children of the Creightons over the years?

8. How did Ross Milton try to ease the burden of the Creighton family?

9. How did war destroy Jenny's dreams?

Across Five Aprils
Chapters 8-9

Vocabulary

mannerism	hoarded	contagion	deserter	forays
impudent	remorse	antagonize		

1. What strategy was the North trying to use to disable the South?

2. What problems were facing the North's war effort from its own side?

3. What caused the soldiers to desert the army? What was meant by, "The war was no breakfas' spell"?

4. How could men avoid serving in the war? What happened to Hig Phillips? Why?

5. Why did the federal registrars come to the Creighton home? How did they treat the family?

6. Why hadn't Jethro experienced the "ridicule of speech" before the war?

7. What words did the author use to describe Eb in such a way that you could visualize him?

8. What fearful decision confronted Jethro? What did he decide to do?

9. The author stated, "It was very simple to lie without words." How did this apply to the story? Give an example from your own life.

10. What did the letter from Lincoln say? What do you think Eb did?

Across Five Aprils
Chapters 10-12

Vocabulary

contemptuous   pandemonium   annals   clemency   amnesty
vindictiveness   tenacity   inevitable

1. What happened to Shadrach in the war?

2. What happiness did Jenny finally find?

3. What was Mr. Lincoln's plan of amnesty? What were the reactions to his idea?

4. Why would it be hard for Mr. Lincoln to win the 1864 election? What events helped to insure his re-election?

5. What was meant in John's letter, "That bullet was not fired by him"? What does this tell you about Bill's feelings of guilt?

6. What had Sherman accomplished? What moral issue was involved?

7. What was on Jethro's mind now that peace was close at hand?

8. What was the irony of April fifth for Jethro?

9. Jethro was given a gift by Shadrach. Describe the gift.

Across Five Aprils
Conclusion and Summary

1. Jethro grew up quickly during the war years. What events contributed to his maturity at such a young age? Which event was most significant to Jethro?

2. While fighting for freedom or other good causes, there are sacrifices. What was the price of freedom paid during the Civil War by the Creightons and others?

3. The war between the States revolved around many sensitive issues. What were some of these issues? How did the issue of loyalty complicate this war?

4. How would the president's assassination threaten the recovery of the nation after the war?

5. Mr. Milton felt that the 13th Amendment would not solve all of America's problems. What problems would need to be resolved for the amendment to be effective?

6. Irene Hunt was personally involved with this book, since it was based on many of her grandfather's experiences. How did the author make you feel personally involved in the story book? What techniques did she use? Give examples.

7. What did you learn about history by reading this book?

8. How did events during this time change the course of history? How would things be different today if the Civil War had not been fought or had been won by the South?

9. A story usually has a setting, a problem, a climax, and an ending. Identify these elements in this story.

10. Choose two characters and tell how they were alike and how they were different.

Across Five Aprils
Activities

1. Draw a map of the Union and Confederate states in the 1860's. Label the states. Indicate the Mason-Dixon line and other significant points of interest mentioned in the book.

2. Make a timeline or chart that shows the major events during the Civil War.

3. Research military guns and equipment. Draw or collect pictures and write a brief description of each.

4. Write a letter to the Creighton family from Bill explaining his reasons for leaving, his war experience, and aspects of his life after the war. Use language and spelling consistent with the family dialect.

5. Research two political figures mentioned in this book. Present information about these persons in a first-person speech or an autobiographical paper, summarizing involvement in the war and related issues.

6. Gather information about Gettysburg. Prepare a model of the battle scene. Write or tape record a description of the battle.

7. Write an essay to explain the 13th Amendment and its impact on Americans in the 1860's and on people today.

8. Locate specific articles written in the 1860's about the Civil war through microfilm, microfiche, or old newspapers. Make a poster using the articles, pictures, or a synopsis of each article.

9. Choose abolitionism, slavery, states rights, or Reconstruction and research it thoroughly. Present your information in an interesting display or report.

10. Pretend that you are living in America prior to the Civil War. With classmates, stage a mock debate on slavery/abolition or states rights.

A Christmas Carol
Charles Dickens

Suggested Reading Level
Grades 6–8

Biography
      Charles Dickens was born in England in 1812. His unfortunate childhood included having to deal with poverty and consequently not receiving the education he wanted and felt he deserved. These experiences made a bitter impression on him and affected his later writings. As a young man he worked as a reporter for a newspaper, which lead to opportunities to write fictional accounts. His works are considered timeless, and many of his writings have been adapted to movies and filmstrips. Other great works include *Tale of Two Cities*, *Great Expectations*, and *David Copperfield*. Dickens died in 1870.

Synopsis
Realistic Fiction

      This timeless classic touches the heart of every reader through the Spirits of Christmas past, present, and future. Scrooge is a single, miserly businessman who shuns family and charities only to find his own wealth brings him little pleasure. Flashbacks into his childhood and young adulthood make him reconsider his lifestyle, but it is the projection of the future that brings about change. A delightful book for the holidays. The vocabulary is difficult at first, but students adapt quickly to Dickens' style.

Themes
1. Spirit of giving and helping others
2. Human interaction and interdependence
3. Nature of happiness
4. Values

Literary Objectives
1. Identify and analyze the flashback technique
2. Identify and analyze the foreshadowing technique
3. Identify the uses of symbolism and irony
4. Identify and analyze the author's style

Companion Titles
1. *The Door in the Wall* – Marguerite de Angeli (human interdependence, spirit of helping others)
2. *Miracles on Maple Hill* – Virginia Sorenson (human interdependence, spirit of giving)
3. *The Pearl* – John Steinbeck (Human interdependence, wealth)

A Christmas Carol
Stave One

Vocabulary

stave	executor	emphatically	ramparts	covetous
palpable	intimation	morose	veneration	liberality
ominous	facetious	tremulous	melancholy	caustic
specter	apparition	dirge		

1. What did Dickens mean by "the wisdom of our ancestors is in the simile"? What was the simile? Why was it important to establish Marley's death?

2. How did Dickens describe Scrooge? What effect did his personality have on his physical features and relationships with other people?

3. What disagreement did Scrooge and his nephew have over the Christmas holiday? What did each one believe?

4. What did the two portly gentlemen want from Scrooge? What was his response? How did his response make him feel?

5. What was Scrooge's reaction to the clerk's request for a holiday?

6. Describe Scrooge's living quarters. Explain what "darkness was cheap and Scrooge liked it" meant.

7. Describe the appearance of Marley's ghost.

8. How did Scrooge try to explain Marley's ghost? Why?

9. What explanation did Marley's ghost give about his appearance before Scrooge? How was his fate after death related to his life? What had he come to tell Scrooge?

10. What warning did the ghost give Scrooge?

11. What did Scrooge see out the window? Why were these ghosts so miserable?

A Christmas Carol

Stave Two

Vocabulary

recumbent	conducive	supplication	vestige	jocund
retentive	condescension	capacious	benevolence	
corroborated	avarice	sordid	tumultuous	

1. What was the first spirit like? What did it represent?

2. Where did the spirit take Scrooge first? What did Scrooge see? What were his reactions?

3. In response to Scrooge's recollection of the caroler, why did the ghost smile "thoughtfully"?

4. Why do you suppose the ghost showed Scrooge little Fan? Who was she? What scene did he show Scrooge?

5. After seeing the Christmas party thrown by the Fezziwigs, the spirit said, "A small matter to make these silly folks so full of gratitude." What did the spirit mean?

6. What was Scrooge's reaction to the happiness generated by Fezziwig?

7. What did Scrooge say regarding the cost of giving happiness? What do you think he wanted to say to his clerk?

8. Why was Scrooge's girlfriend leaving him? How had he changed? How had their relationship changed?

9. The spirit took Scrooge to the home of some boisterous children. How did this scene affect him?

10. What did the light of the Ghost of Christmas Past represent to Scrooge?

A Christmas Carol
Stave Three

Vocabulary

prodigiously   petrification   dogged   facetious   mantled
apoplectic   opulence   officious   declension   credulity
penitence   odious   plaintive   affability   precepts
abject   factious

1. How was Scrooge prepared for the second messenger? Why was he surprised?

2. Describe the second apparition.

3. How did Scrooge greet the Ghost of Christmas Present differently than he had Marley and the first ghost?

4. The second ghost took Scrooge out into the streets on Christmas Day. What special powers did the ghost have?

5. Describe the scene at the Cratchit home. How would you characterize the Cratchit family?

6. What rebuke did the ghost give Scrooge about Tiny Tim's future?

7. What did Scrooge learn by viewing the Cratchit's celebration?

8. Scrooge thought perhaps if he had listened to more music as a child "he might have cultivated the kindness of life for his own happiness." What was he beginning to realize?

9. What did Scrooge's nephew think of him? Why did he bother to invite him to dinner?

10. As they made their many visits that night the ghost "left his blessing and taught Scrooge his precepts." What did this mean?

11. What did the two children clinging to the spirit represent? What was their message for Scrooge?

A Christmas Carol
Stave Four

Vocabulary

shrouded	pendulous	latent	infamous	sepulchres
scrutinize	flaunt	plunder	detestation	bereft
besought	inexorable			

1. What did Scrooge know about the Ghost of Christmas Yet to Come, even though it did not speak?

2. How did Scrooge feel about meeting this ghost?

3. Who was Old Scratch? What did the two businessmen mean by "Old Scratch has got his own at last"?

4. What had the charwoman, laundress, and undertaker's man done? How did they justify their actions?

5. What emotions did they feel about the man's death? Why? How did Scrooge feel about their dealings?

6. What did the ghost show Scrooge about the future of the Cratchits? What impact did Tiny Tim have on their lives?

7. How did Scrooge feel when he read the name on the tombstone?

8. What promises did Scrooge make? Why?

9. What had Scrooge learned?

10. The phantom disappeared into Scrooge's bedpost. Had Scrooge **really** traveled with the ghosts? Explain your answer.

A Christmas Carol
Stave Five

Vocabulary

illustrious   blithe   feign

1. How did Scrooge feel when he realized he was alive?

2. What does the line, "the father of a long, long line of brilliant laughs" tell about Scrooge's changed character?

3. What was Scrooge's first benevolent act?

4. What did Scrooge say to the portly gentleman who had visited him before?

5. The visits from the ghosts made Scrooge determined to bring happiness into the lives of other people, but what changes were made in his disposition? Why do you think this was?

6. Where did Scrooge spend Christmas? What did the group do? Why didn't the author go into greater detail?

7. How did Scrooge treat Bob Cratchit?

8. How did Scrooge change for the future?

9. What was meant by Scrooge "lived upon the Total Abstinence Principle with Spirits ever afterward"?

10. What did it mean to "keep Christmas well"?

A Christmas Carol
Conclusion and Summary

1. What different emotions did each spirit stir in Scrooge? Which specific vision from which spirit had the greatest impact on changing his behavior? Why did it influence him so?

2. If you could interview Charles Dickens today, what would he say is the **true** meaning of Christmas? Do you agree? Why or why not?

3. Dickens' style is vastly different than most contemporary authors you read. Choose three characteristics of his style and describe them. For his message, does his style enhance or detract?

4. From what you saw of his past, what incidents and circumstances made Scrooge the stingy, sour person he was?

5. Which character (the nephew, Tiny Tim, Bob Cratchit, or Marley) embodied the true spirit of Christmas best? Explain. Which character was most like you? Explain.

6. What makes *A Christmas Carol* a timeless classic? Is it the plot? Is it the theme? Is it the style? Defend your answer.

7. Explain the symbolism of the title. What do each of the spirits symbolize?

8. What was the irony of wealth in this novel? Compare and contrast Scrooge's happiness to the Cratchits'.

9. Compare and contrast Scrooge's personality at the beginning of the book with either his nephew or Bob Cratchit.

10. What does this story have to say about: a) relationships b) creating your own happiness c) charity d) wealth? Do you agree?

A Christmas Carol
Activities

1. Watch the movie or a theatrical presentation of *A Christmas Carol*. Compare and contrast it to the book. Write a critical essay discussing the differences.

2. Choose a Christmas story that embodies a theme similar to *A Christmas Carol*. Read it (or part of it) to your class and discuss the meaning and how it compares to *A Christmas Carol*.

3. Dickens' writing reflected the social conditions in England. Research England during the time period between 1830 and 1870. Make a chart that compares life during that time period and now. Make special note of the events or conditions that had particular interest to Dickens.

4. Read James Whitcomb Riley's *Happy Little Cripple*. Read it to your discussion group. Report on the similarities of the two authors' viewpoints about handicapped children.

5. Create a diorama or mural of your favorite scene including Scrooge and a spirit. Write a descriptive paragraph of the scene.

6. Make a model of Scrooge's apartment, place of business, or the Cratchit home. Be sure the decorating and furnishings reflect the personality of the inhabitants and the period in which the story takes place.

7. Research the way the English celebrated Christmas during Dickens' time and now. Report on the changes.

8. Research Charles Dickens. Prepare a report (oral or written) on his life and literary accomplishments. Include a complete bibliography and note cards. If he were alive today, what would he write about? What causes would he support?

9. Read another of Charles Dickens' books. Compare it to this book in terms of literary style and theme.

10. Make a collection of sayings about money, happiness, or something else related to this story. Divide them into two groups according to the ones you agree with and the ones you do not agree with. Explain your choices.

The Grey King
Susan Cooper

Suggested Reading Level
Grades 6-8

Biography
Born in 1935, Susan Cooper enjoyed Welsh tales and legends of King Arthur as she grew up in Buckinghamshire. She was educated at Oxford and listened to lectures of Tolkien and C.S. Lewis. She has lived in the U.S. since 1966 and currently resides in Cambridge, Massachusetts. She was awarded the Newbery Award for *The Grey King* in 1975. It is the third in *The Dark is Rising* series. Other books in this series include *The Dark Is Rising*, *Greenwitch*, and *Silver on the Tree*. She has written several other books for young adults and co-authored the play *Foxfire*.

Synopsis
Fantasy
This story is one in a series of stories about Welsh legends. It appeals to fantasy buffs, mystery lovers, and King Arthur fans. Set in the Welsh countryside where Will goes to recuperate from a severe illness, the mystery unfolds slowly as he makes friends with his aunt and uncle, their hired hand, and a neighbor boy. High adventure, mystery, suspense, and symbolism make for a complicated but well-written novel. While it is not necessary that students have read the other books in this series prior to reading this book, there may be things that they will not fully understand if they have not read the previous books. They will, however, be able to appreciate this fine piece of literature.

Themes
1. Good versus evil
2. Goal setting
3. Human interaction

Literary Objectives
1. Identify and analyze the use of symbolism
2. Identify the climax of the story
3. Analyze the flashback technique
4. Locate clues given in the story

Companion Titles
1. *A Swiftly Tilting Planet* – Madeleine L'Engle (good versus evil)
2. *A Wrinkle in Time* – Madeleine L'Engle (good versus evil)
3. *The Black Cauldron* – Lloyd Alexander (good versus evil)

The Grey King
Prologue and Chapters 1-2
(Prologue – Cadfan's Way)

Vocabulary

prologue   deftly   convalesce   inquisitively   tirade
sagely   enigmatically   dishevelled   shrouded   lychgate
sibilant   malicious   tentative   chaos   unfathomable

1. What is the setting of the story?

2. What happened to Will and Rhys on the way home?

3. What kind of person was Caradog Prichard? What intuitive feelings did Will have about him?

4. How does the reader know this area was steeped in superstition?

5. The word "grey" was used throughout the story to create a mood. Of what does the color grey make you think?

6. What did Will discover in the churchyard? What feelings did this evoke?

7. What did John Rowlands tell Will about Cadfan's Way?

8. Up to this point, what clues do you have that Will may be engaged in a special adventure?

9. Explain Will's encounter with the Welsh sheepdog. What new recollections did this bring back for him?

10. Describe Bran. What connection did Will make between Bran and the recollections he had?

11. Bran told Will he was one of the Old Ones of the Light to hold back the terrible power of the Dark. What did he mean? What did he mean by Dark and Light?

The Grey King
Chapters 3-5
(The Raven Boy – Fire on the Mountain)

Vocabulary

plaintive   prophetic   incredulously   rogue   enmity
malevolence   eccentric   inscrutable   ominous   ludicrous
crescendo

1. What were some of the Signs of the Light? What could be signs of the Light and Dark today?

2. What was Will's quest?

3. How did Bran know of the three lines of Will's poem? How was the poem to help Will?

4. What happened to the ewe? Why was Will worried about the incident?

5. What or who was the Grey King that Will referred to? What did Will feel would happen soon between the Dark and Light?

6. Why was Will surprised when he met Bran's father?

7. How did Will think the sheep had been killed?

8. Explain why the fire symbolized the Dark to Will. What connection did he make between the fire and the Grey King?

9. What emotions would the encounter with Caradog Prichard typically evoke in people? How did Will feel? Why?

10. Describe how the Grey King lured Bran and Will up the mountain and the events that followed.

11. How did Will's special powers compare with those of the Grey King? How, up to this point, have they used these powers?

The Grey King

Chapters 6-7
(Bird Rock – Eyes that See the Wind)

Vocabulary

tentatively	vulnerable	dubious	infinitesimally	inversion
holocaust	treacle	temerity	volition	resonant	ironic
rapt	tremulously			

1. What was High Magic? What was the order of things by which the High Magic would be known?

2. What realization came to Will when he stood under the night sky? What were Will's friends in the sky?

3. Explain what Will and Bran saw and experienced when they went through the last door of the High Magic.

4. The lord told Bran and Will that "only creatures of the earth take from one another. Your own race. . .are the only ones that will ever harm you in the end." What did he foreshadow? What did he mean? Relate this to real life.

5. What did the boys have to do to get the harp?

6. What feelings did Will and Bran experience as they talked to the three lords?

7. What was the worst peril that Will still faced? Why was it dangerous? How would the harp help?

8. Why had the Grey King chosen the beautiful Welsh country for his kingdom?

9. How were Will and Bran saved from the north wind by Cafall and the harp?

10. Describe how Cafall was killed. How did fantasy and reality interact in this incident?

11. Why did John believe Will?

30

The Grey King
Chapters 8–9
(The Girl from the Mountains – The Grey King)

Vocabulary

lee   irresolute   quiescent   belligerence   conspiratorially

bracken   nuance   exultant   stile

1. As a result of the tragedy, how was Bran feeling toward Will? In your opinion, was he justified in feeling this way?

2. What was Will's first reaction to John Rowlands' mention of Cadfan's Way? What did John offer to do? Why do you suppose he didn't want an explanation?

3. How had Bran come to be Owen Davies' son?

4. How was Owen's personality and behavior affected by being Bran's father? Why?

5. Why did Will use magic on Caradog? What was the effect?

6. Explain the incident with the grey fox.

7. What realization did Will have about the power of the Grey King?

8. In your own words, describe the Grey King's appearance.

9. What warning did the Grey King give to Will?

10. What had the warestone enabled the Grey King to do?

11. What did the Grey King say regrading the usefulness of people like Caradog?

12. What was John Rowlands' idea for protecting the dogs?

The Grey King
Chapters 10-11
(The Pleasant Lake - The Warestone)

Vocabulary

humanitarianism	dominant	amiably	ravenous	emanate
inhospitable	bemused	semantics	conciliatory	conundrum
inscrutability	prostrate	petulant	acute	abominably

1. What information did Aunt Jen share about Bran's mother? What was her opinion of Gwen and what she did to Bran?

2. What advice did John Rowlands give Will about the Light? What was Will's response to the advice? How did Will and John's feelings about humans and principles differ?

3. What discovery did John Rowlands make about the dead sheep? What explanation did Will offer?

4. What was the significance of Pleasant Lake? How did this relate to Will's quest?

5. Will felt several feelings as he thought about what might happen next with the Grey King. Are these the feelings you would have felt? Why or Why not? Why do you suppose he wasn't fearful?

6. Why had Bran come to the Lake? How had Bran managed to slow down Caradog's pursuit of Pen?

7. Where did Bran and Will go to hide from Prichard? Was this a good place to hide?

8. Explain what Will did when he discovered Pen under the Grey King's power.

9. What was the warestone? Of what use was it? What warning did Will give Bran about it?

10. How was everything coming together? Why did Will feel that it depended as much on the actions of people as on the Light? Give an example of this.

The Grey King
Chapters 12–13
(The Cottage on the Moor – The Waking)

Vocabulary

penance   disdain   enigma   discordant   innocuous
implacably   self–abasement   annihilation   vulnerable
luminescence   venomous

1. What did Bran think about his father's attitude toward chapel and its effect on their lives?

2. Describe the encounter between Bran and his father. What feelings did each experience? How did the past explain Davies' behavior?

3. What happened to Bran as he discovered a new part of his mind?

4. What puzzled Will about the warestone? How did he use the warestone? What did he see?

5. What was meant by the true nature of Bran Davies, "the child brought out of the past to grow up in the future"? What did Will realize about Bran?

6. Why did Will rush to the lake?

7. What happened when Will met Caradog? Why was Will unable to stop Caradog with his power?

8. Why did the Grey King use an innocent human like Caradog? Why was this risky?

9. Describe the confrontation between Will and the powers of the Grey King in Caradog Prichard.

10. What were the sleepers and who was their leader?

11. Why did the Grey King give up his battle? What effect did this have on Caradog? What happened to the milgwn? Why?

The Grey King
Conclusion and Summary

1. What was the main theme of this book? Explain how it is shown in the book.

2. List several characteristics of both Bran and Will. Which traits were most important in fighting the Dark? Describe how they were different in at least two ways.

3. The climax is an exciting event where the heroes must either win their struggle or be defeated. What is the climax of *The Grey King?* How did you feel at the climax?

4. Will's conflict was his fight against the Dark. What was Bran's conflict? Was his conflict resolved by the end of the story? If so, how?

5. One lesson in *The Grey King* was that we are all vulnerable to evil, and we must be responsible for choosing between good and evil. Give an example of one character from the story and how he chose his destiny. How could you apply this lesson to your life?

6. While this story is a fantasy, and some of the characters have special powers, it also shows the ability of humans to change events through their actions. Describe several instances where this was true.

7. What do you see in our world that might make you think the Dark is still rising? What might make you think the Light is fighting the Dark?

8. Was Will's quest successful? Why or why not?

9. Symbolism is when something (usually tangible) stands for something else (usually intangible). What purpose did the grey foxes serve as literary symbols? What other symbols are used in the story? What do they stand for?

10. Motivation is the reason for acting in a certain way. What was the motivation for Will, Bran, John Rowlands, Caradog Prichard, and Owen Davies?

11. Was Caradog Prichard a victim of circumstance or a master of his own fate? Explain your reasoning?

34

The Grey King

Activities

1. Draw the scene inside Bird Rock as you interpret it. Include the three lords and details from the book.

2. Make an outline for another story in which Will and Bran join forces to fight the Dark.

3. Create a word collage that shows the struggle between good and evil.

4. Study Wales. Prepare a short oral report on the country's geography, climate, and legends. Include a map of the area.

5. Read *The Dark is Rising*, another book by Susan Cooper. Share your interpretation with the class along with a critique of Cooper's style.

6. Prepare a dramatic reading on tape of the poem from which Will and Bran got their clues. Use appropriate sound effects and background music.

7. Make a mural-type map of the places in the story.

8. Write a letter from Will to his parents explaining what has happened during his recuperation. Make sure to include details, but keep in mind how Will must word things so as not to shock or disturb his parents.

9. Compare and contrast the themes of this book to *Star Wars* or *The Black Cauldron* (movies or books). In a three-page essay, establish two points of similarity and two points of difference.

10. Write your own original poem that gives clues to the final fight between the Dark and Light as you envision it.

11. Make a collection of magazine or newspaper articles that show the continuing struggle between the Dark and Light.

12. Make several illustrations for what you feel are the most interesting scenes in this book.

The Incredible Journey
Sheila Burnford

Suggested Reading Level
Grades 6-8

Biography
Sheila Burnford was born in Scotland in 1918. Sheila's own pets were the stimulus for *The Incredible Journey*, published in 1960 and eventually translated into sixteen languages. The book was developed into a motion picture by Walt Disney Studios. Sheila's hobbies include hunting and astronomy.

Synopsis
Realistic Fiction

Three pets (a young Labrador, and old bull terrier, and a Siamese cat) cross the Canadian wilderness in search of their human family. Each animal portrays characteristics that help the trio to survive and succeed in their adventure.

Themes
1. Survival in the wilderness
2. Loyalty
3. Partnership and interdependence

Literary Objectives
1. Analyze the plot, cause and effect, author's style, development of theme
2. Identify personification and evaluate its effectiveness

Companion Titles
1. *Island of the Blue Dolphins* - Scott O'Dell (survival in the wild, human interaction with nature)
2. *The Sign of the Beaver* - Elizabeth G. Speare (survival in the wilderness, loyalty, colonization of a new land, conflict of culture)
3. *The Cay* - Theodore Taylor (survival in the wild, conflict of culture, partnership and interdependence)
4. *Sounder* - William H. Armstrong (animal story)

The Incredible Journey
Chapters 1-2

Vocabulary

burnished   accord   sinew   austerely   docile   parody
incessant   acute

1. How did the three pets come to board with John Longridge?

2. What was the cat's special talent?

3. Which pet had never really adjusted to its new life?

4. Why was it so significant that only the second part of the letter burned?

5. Give a short character description of each pet.

6. What did Mrs. Oakes think had become of the trio?

7. In your opinion, who was the group's leader? Document your answer.

8. Where were the animals going?

9. What is the setting for this story?

The Incredible Journey
Chapters 3-4

Vocabulary

gullet	abhorrent	appease	plaintive	perplexity
facile	succulent	harlequin	forage	ingratiatingly
omen	benevolent			

1. Why did the Lab **not** catch food for himself?

2. Why didn't the bull terrier defend himself?

3. How was the terrier saved from the bears?

4. How did the terrier get food?

5. Describe the sequence of events involving the bears.

6. What made the animals stay in one place for three days?

7. How did each of the three animals behave when they found the Indian camp?

8. What did you learn about the Indians?

9. What kind of sign (omen) was the terrier to the Indians?

The Incredible Journey
Chapters 5-7

Vocabulary

connoisseurs   irresolute   fastidiously   requiem   frugal
heraldic   incongruous   vigilance   enigma   capitulated
voraciously

1. Why didn't this bear cause the trio trouble this time?

2. What kind of pet did the old man have?

3. Why do you feel the dogs did not eat the meal served them?

4. How did the Labrador encourage the others to cross the stream?

5. What happened to the cat?

6. What kind of people were the Nurmis? What evidence can you find in the book to defend your answer?

7. Why did the cat stay so long?

8. Why did the cat leave?

9. What caused the dog fight with the collie?

10. How did the Labrador get porcupine quills in his face?

The Incredible Journey
Chapters 8–9

Vocabulary

impetus	intimidated	discernible	unscathed	gaunt
mutinous	recumbent	travesty	replete	perilous

1. What type of traveler was the cat when he traveled alone?

2. How was the cat saved?

3. How did the terrier and cat assist the Labrador?

4. Why did the bull terrier have a bucket of water thrown on him?

5. How did MacKenzie meet each of the two dogs?

6. It was obvious the MacKenzies loved and understood animals. Give evidence as to how they demonstrated this.

7. Why did the animals leave the MacKenzies'?

8. Why would the rest of the journey be "perilous and exhausting"?

9. Do you think this adventure is realistic? Give evidence to support your position.

The Incredible Journey
Chapters 10–11

Vocabulary

distinctive   recluse   oppressive   incredulous   inconsolable

gallivanting   despondent   raucous

1. Why was Longridge so upset by the animals' disappearance?

2. What did Longridge remember that made him know where the animals had gone?

3. Mrs. Oakes had a favorite animal. Which was it? How do you know?

4. What clues did Longridge have to go on?

5. How did Elizabeth and Peter each approach the problem of the missing animals?

6. What memories sparked Peter's loneliness?

7. Describe the reunion.

8. Why did Tao end the journey with Bodger? Do you feel that this ending was the best or should all three animals have arrived together?

9. According to this book, do animals have emotions and thoughts? Defend your response with examples from the book. What do you think?

10. What things show the animals were resourceful? Courageous? Faithful?

11. What five adjectives would you use to describe the ending?

The Incredible Journey
Conclusion and Summary

1. The story, *The Incredible Journey*, is a warm and loving one. It emphasizes the bond between animals and humans. Do you think the author has described this feeling realistically? Give your opinion based on personal experience and events in the story.

2. Of the three animals, which was the most adventuresome? Use examples from the book to support your choice.

3. Of the three animals, which was the most companionable? Give specific examples to support your choice.

4. How did Longridge's attitude toward animals change through the story from the time he made his offer to care for the animals to the end when he and Peter walked to Lookout?

5. Compare two of the three animals to people you know well. Tell what "personality" traits you feel they have in common. Be sure to describe the people with whom you are making the comparison.

6. If a person had made the same journey as the animal trio, what physical and emotional strengths would they need to be successful?

7. Interpret Walt Whitman's poem, *The Beasts*, as it relates to this story. Use examples from the novel to explain some of Whitman's lines.

8. Other than the ending, write about the part you felt was the most interesting.

9. Most stories have four parts (a setting, a problem, a climax, and an ending). Does this story have all these parts? Identify them.

10. Discuss either loyalty or interdependence as the theme for this story. Give examples from the book to support your choice. Share your own ideas on the topic.

11. What effect did the setting or geography have on the events and characters?

The Incredible Journey
Activities

1. View the Walt Disney movie or a video version of this story. Compare and contrast it to the book in a two minute speech or a two-page paper. Tell which you liked best and give reasons for your preference.

2. Draw a map of Canada, showing the route the pets took across the wilderness. Choose six to eight major events and mark where they occurred.

3. Research Labradors, Siamese cats, or bull terriers. Write a one-page paper and give a two-minute speech on the species. Include its history, characteristics, and a description. Then compare the accuracy of the character in the book to the facts.

4. Make an outline for another incredible journey that could be undertaken either by animals or people. Describe the circumstances that necessitate the journey and include several problems and solutions during the course of the journey.

5. Research Sheila Burnford and discover how her own pets and family experiences played a part in the writing of this novel.

6. Create a new chapter for the book. Make certain that a new problem is created and solved by the end of the chapter. Keep the actions of the animals true to the characterization already presented.

7. Make a poster to advertise the movie version of this story. Use descriptive words and phrases that will make people want to see it. On the back or on another piece of paper, write a brief description of the story.

8. Make a collection of articles or stories about extraordinary behavior or experiences of animals. Display your information in an interesting manner.

9. Write a newspaper article about the return of the three animals.

10. Write a critique of this book for a magazine or newspaper. Devise a rating scale of at least five criteria and use them to judge the book.

Jacob Have I Loved

Katherine Paterson

Suggested Reading Level
Grades 7-9

Biography

Katherine Paterson was born in China in 1932. She was a school teacher and a missionary in Japan. She has been honored with the John Newbery Awards for *Bridge to Terabithia*, *Jacob Have I Loved*, and *The Great Gilly Hopkins*. Some of her other books include *The Master Puppeteer*, *The Sign of the Chrysanthemum*, and *Of Nightingales that Weep*.

Synopsis
Realistic Fiction

This book involves the development of friendships and also the continuing struggle of twin sisters. The two sisters do not get along very well with one another. Louise is boyish in behavior and interests. Caroline is very gifted in music and is a delight to many. The book focuses on the emotional struggles Louise faces growing up. In adulthood, she becomes confident in herself and her gifts. This book requires the understanding of a mature reader.

Themes
1. Development of friendships
2. Family conflicts
3. Coping with unique gifts and talents

Literary Objectives
1. Analyze the character development, symbols, theme
2. Identify qualities of a Newbery Award winner
3. Interpret the use of elements of style, plot, setting

Companion Titles
1. *Bridge to Terabithia* - Katherine Paterson (development of friendships, author study, coping with unique talents and gifts, dealing with death)
2. *From the Mixed-Up Files of Mrs. Basil E. Frankweiler* - E.L. Konigsburg (family conflicts, coping with unique talents and gifts, development of friendships)
3. *The Summer of the Swans* - Betsy Byars (coping with unique talents and gifts, family conflicts, growing up)

Jacob Have I Loved
Rass Island and Chapters 1-2

Vocabulary

brackish	primly	winch	delusions	precarious	undaunted
benevolently	cajoled		lugubriously	polonaise	quaint

1. What was the island and village like where the Bradshaws lived?

2. What did you learn about the narrator in the introduction?

3. Why were Call and the narrator "quite a pair"? How did Call respond to Louise's jokes?

4. Why did Louise think her mother was a "real" lady? What was meant by she's not "an Islander"? Why did this matter?

5. What did the narrator mean by saying she was there "basking in the day"?

6. What was Louise's **natural** and **emotional** relationship with Caroline?

7. What were the circumstances of the twins' birth? How was their birth and the circumstances symbolic of their present lives?

8. How could Louise be offended by not having been a worry to her parents?

9. What was meant by "Caroline is the kind of person other people sacrifice for as a matter of course"?

10. What was to blame for the change in Louise the year she turned thirteen?

Jacob Have I Loved
Chapters 3-6

Vocabulary

petulant   pretentious   caricature   melancholy   indict
improvise   feigned   remorse

1. How did the attack on Pearl Harbor affect Louise and Caroline?

2. What was Louise's suggestion about Christmas to Mr. Rice? What was she feeling when she made that statement? How did her classmates react? Do you think she was right? Why or why not?

3. How could being with Caroline make Louise feel alone?

4. Why did Louise have so many fantasies?

5. Was Caroline gifted? Tell why or why not. Did Louise have gifts or talents? Explain.

6. What was the mystery of the stranger?

7. Why was Louise worried about Call and the Captain?

8. Why did Louise feel guilty about hating Caroline?

9. What did Louise begin to do with the money she earned? What was her plan for this money?

Jacob Have I Loved
Chapters 7–10

Vocabulary

integrity   concession   futile   saboteur   aberrations

paregoric   intrigue

1. How had Louise and Call's relationship with the Captain changed?

2. According to Louise, how was her physical and spiritual health?

3. How did Louise describe February? Why was August a "dream killer"?

4. Why was it so important to Louise for the stranger to be Hiram, an islander who had escaped?

5. How did Louise and the Captain's relationship change that day? What two events made it change?

6. How did Call and Louise know Captain was Hiram Wallace? What surprising fact did the Captain know about Trudy?

7. What was the original plan to get rid of the cats? Why was this plan abandoned?

8. How did Caroline help with the cat problem? How did Louise react to the solution?

9. What one thing did the hurricane accomplish?

Jacob Have I Loved
Chapters 11–14

Vocabulary

capricious   blanche   piously   shrapnel   destitute
perfunctorily

1. What was Captain's reaction to the damage to his house? What did Louise think about the Captain's reaction?

2. How had Louise begun to think of the Captain?

3. What had Louise decided about hands? When Caroline used Louise's hand lotion, why did Louise react the way she did?

4. Why did Caroline, along with Call and Louise, go see the Captain? What happened when they saw the Captain?

5. What happened the last time Caroline, Call, and Louise visited the Captain?

6. Why did Louise cry at Auntie Braxton's funeral?

7. What were the girls' reactions to Grandma's rampage? What is Grandma's role in the plot of the story?

8. How was Call changing? Why did that change make Call and Louise grow apart?

9. What was the last straw for Louise that occurred upon the Captain's visit?

10. What is the significance of Romans 9:13, "Jacob have I loved, but Esau have I hated"? (Answer only after discussion)

Jacob Have I Loved

Chapters 15–17

Vocabulary

contemptuously   staccato   inanities   extricated

1. Why had the Captain's decision hurt Louise so much?

2. Who was the speaker of the quote from Romans 9:13? How did this discovery affect Louise?

3. How did Mother deal with Caroline's good fortune?

4. What did Louise mean when she thought, "You don't come home after two years and suddenly inform your mother that she's dying"?

5. How did the water nibble away the land and the "war nibble away our souls"?

6. Why did Louise quit going to church?

7. Why was Louise, while working the oyster beds with her Father, experiencing the happiest days of her life?

8. How was Louise like the oysters? Give another simile to describe Louise.

9. What did Louise mean when she said, "It was not the European war that concerned her"? What war plagued her?

10. What news did Call have? How did Louise feel about the news?

11. What did Louise find out about her grandmother and the Captain? How did this change her feelings somewhat about her grandmother?

12. What did the Captain tell Louise he had always known about her? What was her ambition?

Jacob Have I Loved
Chapters 18-20

Vocabulary

contentious   rancor   petulantly   renunciation

1. What confused Louise about her mother? Why had her mother come to Rass Island?

2. What did Louise discover about her own dreams in that conversation?

3. What word finally allowed Louise to begin to build herself a soul? What is the author's definition of a soul? What is your definition?

4. What blow did Louise receive at the University of Maryland? Would that happen today? Explain.

5. How did Louise cope? Where and why did she move her crab pots, and how did she change her goals?

6. Compare and contrast the mountain-locked valley and the island.

7. Why had Louise, who could have had anything she wanted, come to the valley?

8. What did Louise mean when she said that Joseph was the kind of man who would sing to the oysters?

9. Why was it Caroline, and not Louise, who attended the funeral? How did this further develop the theme of the book?

10. What did Louise experience that night when the twins were born? What changes did she hope to make?

Jacob Have I Loved
Conclusion and Summary

1. Louise was a very complex character. How does the author communicate that? List Louise's strengths and weaknesses. How did she change?

2. What is this author's message about war? How can a war exist within a person as well as between people? Explain the war that was going on inside Louise.

3. What is important about someone having a feeling of self-worth? What is important about helping someone have a soul? Give personal examples and examples from the book.

4. What does this author say about girls, boys, and the opportunities in life? Should Louise have tried to bloom where she was planted (on Rass Island) or go away? Defend your response.

5. Do you feel that Caroline deserved Louise's hatred? Why or why not?

6. Re-read the beginning section, "Rass Island," and explain why you feel the author chose to put this at the beginning rather than at the end of the book.

7. Describe all the ways Louise felt she was robbed by Caroline. What intangible things did she think she lost to her sister?

8. What did this book have to say about: a) sibling rivalry b) love c) opportunity d) personal strength e) talents f) cycles?

9. What were the five most important things that happened in this story? How did they help in building the plot? What events allowed the plot to make a complete cycle?

10. What did the last paragraph in the book mean? What do you think will be in Louise's future? What events allowed the plot to make a complete cycle?

11. What was the conflict in this story? How was the conflict resolved by the end of the book?

Jacob Have I Loved
Activities

1. Make a circular timeline of the events in Louise's life. Limit yourself to between six and eight events.

2. Pretend you are writing Caroline's diary. Pick three scenes from the book and describe them from her point of view.

3. Research Katherine Paterson's life and literary accomplishments. Share what you find with the class.

4. Read another of Katherine Paterson's books. Compare and contrast the books, focusing mainly on the differences and similarities of the main characters in the two books.

5. Define a time capsule and then decide what Dad, Mom, Grandma, Louise, Caroline, Captain, Call, and Auntie Braxton would put in one. Be able to tell why you chose each item for each person.

6. Write titles for each of the chapters in the book.

7. Write a description of how an island is formed. Find information on the erosion as described by Call when he said that in two years they had lost an acre. Is this loss typical of most islands? Why? Why not?

8. Create a poem, essay, or song to share your feelings or ideas about this story.

9. Research crabs and/or oysters. Share your information in a written or oral report. Include illustrations.

10. Research twins and report on the most recent findings.

11. Make a rating scale of at least five criterion and use it to evaluate this book. Use this evaluation to write a critique of the book, discussing its good points, bad points, and why people your age might enjoy reading it.

Jonathan Livingston Seagull
Richard Bach

Suggested Reading Level
Grades 7-8

Biography
Richard Bach was born in 1936 in Illinois. He has six children, one whose name is Jonathan. He served as a pilot in the U.S. Air Force. He is a free-lance writer with several books to his credit. *Jonathan Livingston Seagull* was filmed in 1973. Mr. Bach said the reader must interpret this book for his/her own meaning. He says this story came to him in a vision.

Synopsis
Fantasy

This seemingly simple tale is about a seagull who is ostracized by the flock for wanting to achieve perfection in flight instead of worrying about mundane tasks like fishing or eating. Jonathan is intrinsically motivated to do well, much to the disgust of the rest of the flock. Symbolically this parable can be bibliotherapy for dealing with giftedness or differentness. While the book is short and the reading is not difficult, the symbolism and theme take a mature reader to adequately understand and analyze.

Themes
1. Coping with unique abilities
2. Goal setting
3. Meaning of life
4. Dealing with conflict
5. Coping with death

Literary Objectives
1. Analyze the use of text and photographs
2. Identify and analyze the use of symbolism
3. Identify and analyze the author's purpose
4. Identify and analyze the use of personification

Companion Titles
1. *The Little Prince* - Antoine de Saint Exupery (meaning of life, dealing with loss)
2. *Jacob, Have I Loved* - Katherine Paterson (coping with unique abilities)
3. *Tuck Everlasting* - Natalie Babbitt (life and death)
4. *The Black Cauldron* - Lloyd Alexander (good versus evil, price of freedom)
5. *A Wrinkle in Time* - Madeleine L'Engle (coping with unique abilities)

Jonathan Livingston Seagull
Part I

Vocabulary

resolutions   terminal   aerobatics   irresponsibility
solitude   intone

1. The author explains what sets Jonathan apart from the other gulls. Why was Jonathan different?

2. How did Jonathan's mother and father feel about his flying? What did they recommend?

3. What victory did Jonathan accomplish? Why was the victory short-lived?

4. What changes did Jonathan have to make to be a normal seagull?

5. After vowing to be a normal gull, what did Jonathan learn about flying? What happened to his vow?

6. How did Jonathan expect the flock to react to his new accomplishment? Why?

7. For what reasons was Jonathan called to Stand to Center? What did this mean?

8. What was Jonathan's explanation? How did the flock respond to his explanation?

9. Once on his own, what did Jonathan learn about flying and life? Do you agree with his explanation of a short life?

10. What do you think was happening to Jonathan at the end of Part I?

11. Have you ever felt different or had high expectations for yourself, like Jonathan? Explain your situation.

Jonathan Livingston Seagull
Part II

Vocabulary

aeronautics   telepathy   inverted   enfeebled   empowered
scorn   exhorting   adept   chaos

1. What were Jonathan's first disappointments and questions when he first entered heaven?

2. What was different in this new life? What was the important thing in this life?

3. What was Sullivan's explanation to Jonathan about why there were not more gulls?

4. Sullivan said, "Learn nothing, and the next world is the same as this one, all the same limitations and lead weights to overcome." What did Jonathan have to overcome?

5. What advice did Chiang give Jonathan? Do you agree or disagree? Why?

6. Describe what happened when Jonathan was able to reach the perfection of speed? Why was he able to learn so quickly?

7. What did Chiang say was the next step? What did he say would be the most powerful and fun?

8. What desire did Jonathan develop as he practiced his kindness lessons? Why did Jonathan want to go back to the flock?

9. Explain "the gull sees farthest that flies highest." Relate this to Jonathan's experience.

10. How did Sullivan feel about Jonathan's desire to return to Earth? What did Jonathan tell Sully about missing each other?

11. What had happened to Fletcher? Compare him to Jonathan.

12. What happened when Fletcher met Jonathan?

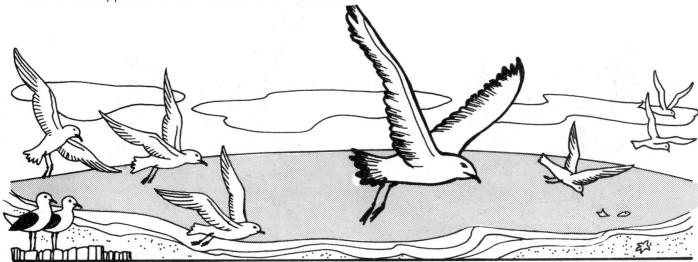

Jonathan Livingston Seagull
Part III

Vocabulary

anguish   gamely   critique   wry   furtive   divine
idolize   transparent   quizzically

1. What two things did all of Jonathan's students have in common?

2. What was Jonathan having trouble getting across to his students?

3. How did the flock feel about Jonathan's students? How did the Elder Gull tell them to treat the outcasts?

4. What did Jonathan and his pupils do despite the treatment?

5. What did Jonathan tell the other gulls when they said that he was a special gull? Do you agree? Why or why not?

6. What happened to Fletcher?

7. Why wasn't Fletcher dead? What reaction did the flock have?

8. How could Jonathan love the gulls who wanted to destroy him?

9. What did Jonathan mean when he said, "Don't you think there might be other flocks that need an instructor more than this one, that's on its way toward the light"?

10. What happened to Jonathan?

11. How did Fletcher face his new responsibilities?

Jonathan Livingston Seagull
Conclusion and Summary

1. Jonathan Livingston Seagull learned a lesson in this story, then taught it to Fletcher. This lesson is the theme or main idea. In your own words, tell what the theme of this story is. Document with examples or quotes.

2. Jonathan risked the acceptance of the flock to strive to do his best. Compare this to a situation in your own life. Describe a situation when you took risks to strive toward a personal goal or achievement.

3. Explain why Jonathan wanted to fly faster and higher. What did this represent for him at the beginning of the book and at the end of the book?

4. What is your idea of a model teacher? Compare Jonathan with this model. Was he a good teacher? Explain your decision.

5. Describe at least three of Jonathan's characteristics. Give an example of each from the book.

6. What was the author's outlook on death?

7. The author used a seagull to tell a message. Give three good reasons why you think he did this. Would another character have been as effective? Why or why not?

8. What do you hope to accomplish someday? What did you learn from this story that you could apply to meeting this goal?

9. What problems did Jonathan have with the other gulls? What problems might someone with special talents have with other people?

10. According to Jonathan, what is the meaning of life? Can this be generalized to people? How?

11. What intangible ideas are shown in this book?

12. Explain how this book could be read and enjoyed by people of many different ages.

Jonathan Livingston Seagull
Activities

1. Give an oral or written report on sea gulls. Research their capabilities and weaknesses. Explain their habits and habitats as they relate to this novel.

2. Write an interesting but simplified version of the story that younger children could understand. Read this book to a group of younger students. Use dramatization and visuals to make it interesting.

3. Read *Illusions* by Richard Bach and write a one to two page essay comparing and contrasting the style and theme with *Jonathan Livingston Seagull*.

4. Watch the movie version of *Jonathan Livingston Seagull* or listen to the recording of the soundtrack. Write a one to two page essay giving your opinions about the quality of the interpretation and the authenticity as it relates to the author's purpose.

5. Find two or three poems that have the same theme as *Jonathan Livingston Seagull*. Read them to the class with expression, stating why each poem was chosen.

6. Draw a mural depicting the characters and steps Jonathan went through to reach perfection.

7. Write a journal entry telling how you and your social and academic peers compare to Jonathan and the flock.

8. Prepare a multi-media program that interprets the theme of *Jonathan Livingston Seagull*. Limit your program to one to three minutes.

9. Create a word collage that shows your ideas about perfection, meeting goals, love, or some other idea that was presented in this book.

10. Write a poem about Jonathan Livingston Seagull and the principles that guided his behavior. Choose appropriate music to accompany your poem. Read it with the musical background.

The Pearl
John Steinbeck

Suggested Reading Level
Grades 7-9

Biography
John Steinbeck was born in California in 1902. He often worked on difficult jobs so he could better understand people and the lives they led. He won the Pulitzer Prize in 1940 for *The Grapes of Wrath*. He was also awarded the Nobel Prize for Literature. Other works include *The Red Pony* and *Travels with Charlie*. He died in December 1968.

Synopsis
Realistic Fiction

This classic novel tells the story of a poor fisherman who finds a coveted pearl, the pearl of the world. However, danger and misfortune follow this family instead of the great happiness and security that this treasure should have given. The reader must wrestle with what things in life are to be treasured.

Themes
1. Good versus evil
2. Dealing with death
3. Poverty versus wealth
4. Prejudice

Literary Objectives
1. Analyze the character development, symbols, and theme
2. Identify and analyze the qualities of a classic
3. Interpret the use of elements of style, theme, plot setting
4. Identify and analyze the techniques of irony and imagery

Companion Titles
1. *A Taste of Blackberries* – Doris Buchanan Smith (dealing with death, development of friendships, peer pressure, family conflicts)
2. *The Cay* – Theodore Taylor (dealing with death, prejudice, human interaction with nature, conflict of culture)
3. *Sounder* – William Armstrong (prejudice, dealing with death)

The Pearl
Chapter 1

Vocabulary

detachment	pulque	feinted	plaintively	lymphatic
avarice	consolation	indignant	suppliant	

1. Describe two different songs that Kino and/or Juana heard. What did the songs symbolize?

2. What clues do you get about the setting of the story in the first chapter?

3. Explain the statement, "They had spoken once, but there is not need for speech if it is only habit anyway."

4. What happened to the baby? Why was this dangerous?

5. List the different things the scorpion could have represented.

6. Describe the feeling Kino and Juana must have felt when the scorpion struck.

7. What kind of a person was Juana? Explain the real reasons why the doctor would not come to the brush houses.

8. When Kino and Juana walked into town, many people judged them by their appearance. What was their assessment? Compare this to a real life situation in today's world.

9. By what did they judge the doctor? What was their opinion of him?

10. Explain what the doctor implied when he said, "I am a doctor, not a veterinary."

11. What was meant by, "A wave of shame went over the whole procession"?

The Pearl
Chapter 2

Vocabulary

estuary   mirage   telescopically   bulwark   undulating
perceptible   speculatively   hummock   deftly

1. What did the canoes represent? What things do people have today that hold the same meaning?

2. Why did the Indians not always trust what they thought they saw?

3. What were the social expectations of a man in regards to caring for his family?

4. Why was the poultice not as good as a doctor's treatment in Juana's eyes?

5. What did the author mean by, "The minds of people are as unsubstantial as the mirage of the gulf"?

6. The author uses descriptive language to create images for the reader. He makes the reader feel as if he or she is really seeing the scene. Refer to the section concerning the pearl bed. How were the oysters and the oyster beds described?

7. What steps did Kino follow to obtain the pearls?

8. Why was it not good to want a thing too much?

9. What did Kino find?

10. How did Kino react to his great find?

The Pearl
Chapter 3

Vocabulary

judicious	precipitated	distillate	incandescence
disparagement	almsgiver	lucent	confirmation
subjugation	furtive		

1. Chapter 3 began with a simile. What two things were being compared? Explain in your own words.

2. How did the people in the village view Kino's discovery? What did they want from his good fortune?

3. What were some of the things Kino thought the pearl would buy for him?

4. The author said, "For it is said that humans are never satisfied, that you give them one thing and they want something more." If this is true, give examples of this in the world today. If you feel this is not true, tell how people are satisfied with their position and wealth in life.

5. Why was it so important that Coyotito have an education?

6. Why did the doctor come to Kino's house? What was his real motive? Were Kino's feelings toward him justified? Explain.

7. Kino was beginning to feel fearful. Why?

8. What happened that night? What was Kino compared to during the attack?

9. What conflicting feelings did Kino and Juana have about the pearl? Who do you think was right? Explain.

10. How could something as beautiful and good as the pearl bring evil into people's lives?

The Pearl
Chapter 4

Vocabulary

countenanced   insubstantial   stalwart   benign   legerdemain
understatement   contemptuous   collusion   lethargy

1. How were the pearl buyers organized? Was this the right thing for them to do? Why?

2. What was the vision? What was its symbolism? What did the people believe about ambition and improving one's life?

3. What happened when Kino went to sell the pearl? Did Kino understand the game that the buyers were playing? Explain.

4. How had Kino lost one world but not gained another?

5. What game was Juan Tomas referring to when he spoke to Kino about going to the city and selling the pearl?

6. Compare and contrast the characteristics of Kino in the beginning of the book with some of the attributes or traits he exhibited in Chapter 4.

7. What effect did the second attack have on Juana and Kino's feelings about the pearl?

8. What reason was Juana given to accept Kino's plan? Was it an acceptable one to you? Why or why not?

The Pearl
Chapter 5

Vocabulary
lament   mangroves

1. What was Juana going to do with the pearl? What did Juana hope to accomplish? Would it have made a difference?

2. Irony is the incongruity between what might be expected and what actually occurs. What is ironic about Juana's actions concerning the pearl?

3. Do you think Kino was justified in treating Juana the way he did?

4. What emotions would you have felt if you had been Juana? Why was she not angry with Kino?

5. Why did Juana say they had to go away?

6. How did Kino feel when he found his boat had been ruined? How would you have felt?

7. How was Kino like an animal?

8. What other misfortune befell Kino and Juana?

9. How did Juan Tomas help his brother?

10. Why was Kino unwilling to give up the pearl?

11. What did Kino mean when he said that the pearl had become his soul? Can you imagine something becoming that important to you? Explain.

The Pearl
Chapter 6

Vocabulary

monotonously   pelted   covert   resinous   monolithic
irresolution   escarpment   petulant   germane   malignant

1. What visions did Kino see in the pearl? How were they different from what he wanted to see?

2. Do you think Kino did all he could to protect his family? Explain.

3. What kind of people were hunting Kino?

4. What happened at the water hole?

5. Explain why Kino's desire for a rifle was significant.

6. Compare and contrast Juana's feeling at the time of the scorpion with her feelings at this point in the story.

7. What was the climax? What was so ironic about it?

8. How did the townspeople respond when Kino and Juana returned to the village?

The Pearl
Conclusion and Summary

1. What examples of symbolism are used in this novel.

2. How does the story demonstrate the theme of good versus evil?

3. Explain how differences between the privileges of the wealthy and the poor are shown in *The Pearl*. Describe another situation where people could be taken advantage of because of their lack of knowledge.

4. Kino's boat represented stability and the future. Why was this so? What things represent stability and the future in your life?

5. Kino and Juana did not always communicate with words. What ways were used by them to express feelings and thoughts without actually speaking? What nonverbal ways do people you know use to communicate?

6. How did the author use the metaphor of song to explain feelings?

7. What does the story say about ignorance, suspicion, ambition, greed, or good fortune? Do you agree?

8. Give examples of superstitions from this story. What effect did they have on the characters?

9. How did Kino's feelings change throughout the story? Was the pearl the only cause of these changes?

10. The author stated that "if this story is a parable, everyone takes his own meaning from it." What meaning did the story have for you?

11. What one word summarizes your feelings about the ending?

The Pearl
Activities

1. Create a diorama or illustration of a favorite scene from the book.

2. With a small group of classmates, act out a scene from the novel. Write your script to show emotions.

3. Create a mural or timeline to show events from the book. Include at least six significant scenes.

4. Write a one to three-page report about pearls. Tell the uses, describe the areas where they are usually found, and describe how they are harvested.

5. Write a poem or essay showing your feelings about one of the concepts presented in this book.

6. Write a short dialogue showing what the people of the village might have said about Kino and Juana when they returned.

7. Research and write a brief report on John Steinbeck and his writings. Explain what impact his personal experiences had on his writing.

8. Compare and contrast the story, *Sea of Cortez* by John Steinbeck, and this novel.

9. Make a map of lower California and locate places from the story. Include a brief report on the geography, climate, and natural resources.

10. Write a critique of this book for a magazine or newspaper. Be fair in your evaluation. State the criterion you used to evaluate the book.

A Swiftly Tilting Planet
Madeleine L'Engle

Suggested Reading Level
Grades 6-8

Biography
Madeleine L'Engle taught for many years. She kept a journal from which she would use ideas. She usually wrote about places she had visited or knew well. *A Wrinkle in Time* won the Newbery Award in 1963. Another companion title is *A Wind in the Door*. Titles such as *The Moon by Night*, *The Arm of the Starfish*, and *The Young Unicorns* are very popular with young audiences. As of 1986 she was still making personal appearances. She lives in New York City with her husband who is a TV actor.

Synopsis
Science Fiction
This story is a sequel to *A Wrinkle in Time* and *A Wind in the Door*. It is not dependent on either of these for understanding. Charles Wallace is now older and with his unicorn Gaudior is in battle against the evil Madog Branzillo. His sister Meg can give him help by kything. The whole family becomes involved in the prevention of war as Charles goes back through time to change events that will affect the future.

Themes
1. Cause and effect
2. Development of friendships
3. Family relationships
4. Dealing with unique abilities
5. Good versus evil

Companion Titles
1. *A Wrinkle in Time* – Madeleine L'Engle (social implications of technology, dealing with unique abilities)
2. *The White Mountains* – John Christopher (social implications of technology, development of friendships)
3. *Mrs. Frisby and the Rats of Nimh* – Robert C. O'Brien (social implications of technology)

A Swiftly Tilting Planet

Chapters 1-2

Vocabulary

burgeoning   morosely   coup d'etat   retribution   defoliation
antiballistic   ironic   taciturn   simultaneous   brusque
havoc   clarion   imploringly   acquiescence

1. Describe each character: Meg O'Keefe, Charles Wallace, Mrs. O'Keefe, Mrs. Murry.

2. How was the Murry family different from other families?

3. To which member of her family was Meg closest? Why?

4. Why did the President call Mr. Murry?

5. For what reasons was Branzillo starting a war? Was this good logic? What would be the effects?

6. What was Patrick's rune? What effect did it have on Charles Wallace? What did it reveal about Mrs. O'Keefe?

7. What was kything?

8. How did Ananda join the household? What did her name mean?

9. Explain what happened when Charles Wallace went on his walk.

10. Explain what Charles Wallace might have meant when he said, "We haven't done all that well by our planet, have we?"

A Swiftly Tilting Planet
Chapters 3-4

Vocabulary

antecedents	cacophony	primordial	inexorably	dissonant
languorously	abominable	spontaneity	pungent	luminosity
acrid	paroxysms	soothsayers	delirium	

1. What did Meg experience when she returned to her room?

2. Where did Gaudior take Charles Wallace?

3. Explain the change in setting. What does the author do to make it dramatic?

4. What did Gaudior and Charles Wallace learn about each other?

5. What was Charles Wallace's mission? Why would it be difficult for him?

6. Who was Harcels? What was he like?

7. What did Charles Wallace experience within Harcels? Why was he given this experience?

8. What was a Projection? What happened while Gaudior and Charles were blown into a Projection?

9. Why did Madoc not stay in his homeland and become king?

10. Why did Reschal make Madoc relive his brother's death before marrying Zyll?

11. Who arrived at the wedding celebration? Why was Madoc surprised?

12. Who or what was Echthroi? What power did it have?

A Swiftly Tilting Planet
Chapters 5-6

Vocabulary

amity   imperiously   bulbous   derisively   chided
veritable   contretemps   vindictive   desist   quell
deign   blaspheme

1. What did Gwydyr want of Madoc and the Wind People? Why?

2. Explain the battle between Madoc and Gwydyr. Who won? How?

3. Madoc saw two visions in the puddle. What did they mean?

4. What did Meg find out from the encyclopedia and reference books?

5. What was the relationship between Brandon and Zylle?

6. What special ability did Brandon possess? How was this viewed by his family and Zylle's family?

7. What visions did Brandon see?

8. How had Pastor Mortmain changed the community?

9. How did Richie and Zylle represent the union of two legends?

10. What warning did Maddok give Brandon?

11. How was the hanging stopped? Did people's feelings change?

12. Why did Ritchie and Zylle return to Wales? What new union would bring the two groups together in their absence?

A Swiftly Tilting Planet
Chapters 7–8

Vocabulary

suppositions	buffeted	testily	futile	draughts
luminosity	nuptials	posthumously		inconsequentially
evocative				

1. What is the significance of the chapter titles?

2. What were the Echthroi trying to prevent?

3. What connection did Charles Wallace make between Madoc and Branzillo?

4. What did Charles Wallace now understand about the Echthroi?

5. Where were Charles Wallace and Gaudior trying to go in Chapter 7? Where did they end up?

6. How had Charles Wallace and Gaudior been physically affected by their ordeal? How were they healed?

7. Who were Chuck and Beezie? What was their connection with the characters who have been introduced so far?

8. What story did Chuck and Beezie's grandmother tell them?

9. What special abilities did Chuck have?

10. Describe Matthew Maddox's writings. What effect did he have on Mr. Maddox?

11. What problem did Chuck and Beezie's father have with his business? Why?

12. Chuck's father died. What premonitions did Chuck have that this would happen or had happened?

A Swiftly Tilting Planet
Chapters 9-10

Vocabulary

psychiatry	inevitability	bemusedly	aquiline	ingrate
holocaust	corroborate	rampant		

1. Why did Mrs. O'Keefe go over to the Murrys' house? What new information did she share? What questions did it raise for Meg?

2. What was in Mr. Maddox's strongbox? What clues did it hold?

3. Explain the passage from Chapter 9, "The present was so bleak that all three found relief in living in the past."

4. Why did Beezie want to use the rune?

5. What was Duthbert really like? How did he treat the children? What did he do to Chuck?

6. What was meant by the **two** stones in the cemetery?

7. Why was Charles Wallace chosen for this mission? Give three reasons.

8. How did the Echthroi try to trick Charles Wallace? What had he learned that enabled him to resist it?

9. What did Meg discover that was important to know?

10. How did Chuck's life change after the accident? Why wouldn't he tell his mother about his eyes?

11. Interpret the events at the end of Chapter 10.

A Swiftly Tilting Planet
Chapters 11–12

Vocabulary

vicariously	debonair	ostentatious	facade	arduous
malingering	indubitably	adamant	conniving	volition
adulation	fratricide	dissonance		

1. What injuries did Matt and Bran have? How did they receive them?

2. What happened to Bran's soul during the war? What did he learn about men?

3. What was Bran's plan? Why did he make this arrangement?

4. Explain Bran's meaning when he said, "God withdrew from our battlefields."

5. Matthew told Zillah about finishing a book. What was it about?

6. Matthew told why his story would be so important. Why?

7. What interconnections did Matthew have after Bran's letter?

8. Why did Zillah have to go to South America?

9. What event changed the relationships between the people of Vespugia? How?

10. What was the final result of Charles Wallace and Gaudior's adventure?

11. How had Charles Wallace and Gaudior changed history? Do you think it was worth the risk?

A Swiftly Tilting Planet
Conclusion and Summary

1. What does the title *A Swiftly Tilting Planet* symbolize?

2. What theme did the author project about human's treatment of each other and the environment? Do you agree? Explain.

3. What did Madeleine L'Engle express about the impact of the past on the present and future? Do you agree? Explain.

4. Charles Wallace was chosen for this mission. What qualities did he possess that made him the one to go back in time to change the present? What did he have to learn?

5. Matthew Maddox's books were entitled *Once More United* and *The Horn of Joy*. What did the titles tell you about the themes of the books?

6. In each story or set of characters Charles Wallace experienced, there were good and evil characters. Why do you suppose the author did this? What was she saying?

7. How were things meant to be? Why didn't things always turn out that way?

8. What should be done now and in the future to prevent evil from overshadowing good?

9. What did Charles Wallace mean when he said Mrs. O'Keefe had placed herself between the powers of darkness? Was she a hero?

10. Summarize the following stories:
    Chapters 3–5   Madoc, Zyll, Gwydyr, Reschal
    Chapter 6   Maddok, Zylle, Brandon, Ritchie, Rev. Mortmain
    Chapters 7–10   Chuck, Beezie, Mr. & Mrs. Maddox, Duthbert Mortmain
    Chapters 11–12   Matthew, Bran, Zillah, Gedder, Gwen

A Swiftly Tilting Planet
Activities

1. Write your own song or poem to reflect your feelings about one of the ideas in this book.

2. Research ESP and other para-psychological phenomenon. Share your information in an oral or written report.

3. Research the Salem witch trials. Explain what brought them about, when they occurred, and why they were stopped.

4. Draw the star-watching rock in each of the different time settings.

5. Make a detailed diorama or illustration of the place where Gaudior took Charles Wallace to be healed. Include details of the hatching grounds.

6. Make a real timeline of the year 1865. Label important dates and events. Tell which of the events related directly to the themes of *A Swiftly Tilting Planet*.

7. Memorize and recite the rune from this story. Find two other runes. Tell where you found them and their significance.

8. Using maps and/or transparencies of the world, show the locations of the four stories in Chapter 9. Tell how each are related to one another.

9. Create a word collage that illustrates good versus evil.

10. What could you do to make a positive change in the future of the world? Make a list of ideas. Choose one and make a plan of action.

76

Ten Little Indians
Agatha Christie

Suggested Reading Level
Grades 7–8

Biography
Agatha Christie was born in England on September 15, 1890 and died there in 1976 after publishing over eighty books. Among her most remembered titles were *Murder on the Orient Express*, written in 1934 and a play *The Mousetrap*, written in 1952. A distinguished author and dramatist, Christie earned the Mystery Writers of America Grand Master Award in 1954, and *Witness for the Prosecution* won the New York Drama Critics Circle Award for best foreign play in 1955. Christie received an honorary doctorate in literature from the University of Exeter in 1961.

Synopsis
Mystery

Ten individuals are all invited under vague or unusual circumstances to spend a short vacation on Indian Island in Devon, England. Soon it is discovered that the common bond of these ten guests is their mysterious past; the probable involvement in a murder that was beyond the law, a murder for which they have paid no penalty. One by one, each guest is murdered and the reader tries to identify the murderer. This is one of Christie's best and most suspenseful works. Reading this story requires mental gymnastics; and for those who are stumped, the epilogue and concluding manuscript satisfies one's curiosity. This book includes some profanity and racial slurs.

Themes
1. Guilt as a form of justice
2. Righteousness prevails
3. Dealing with injustice
4. Struggle for survival

Literary Objectives
1. Identify and analyze the technique of foreshadowing
2. Identify and analyze the elements of mystery and suspense
3. Identify climax
4. Analyze character development

Companion titles
1. *The Westing Game* – Ellen Raskin (elements of a mystery)
2. *The Wolves of Willoughby Chase* – Joan Aiken (struggle for survival, elements of a mystery)
3. *The Railway Children* – E. Nesbit (dealing with injustice)

Ten Little Indians
Chapters 1–2

Vocabulary

sine qua non   deportment   plaintively   pacifically
recumbent   surreptitious   imperceptibly   disparagingly
natal   malevolence   forage   fraternizing   apparition
monotonous   luxuriate

1. Why did this mystery have a cast of characters at the beginning?

2. What is a soldier-of-fortune? How did it apply in this story?

3. What uncertainties and mysteries surrounded Indian Island?

4. What warning did Mr. Blore receive? What did it foreshadow?

5. In your opinion, which character seemed the most intriguing? Why?

6. What was Mr. Narracott's impression of the guests? What did he think about the owners of Indian Island?

7. What were some of the guests' first impressions of Indian Island?

8. Why did Vera feel disturbed? What poem did she find? How did its message affect her?

9. What did you learn about the judge and Mr. Armstrong? What is the significance of this?

10. Emily was reading the *Bible*. What did the quote foretell?

11. What clues have you been given up to this point?

Ten Little Indians
Chapters 3-5

Vocabulary

caustic   adroitly   verisimilitude   iniquitous   exonerated
differential   dissentient   capricious   hypocrite
reconnaissance   decorous   overvehement   rancor

1. How was the setting particulary appropriate for this story?

2. What was the purpose of the recording? With what did the voice charge the guests?

3. What were some of the various reactions to the recorded accusations?

4. What evidence did the guests present regarding their presence at Indian Island? From this, what conclusion did the judge make?

5. Each person was connected to the death of another person yet did not feel responsible. What rationalizations did they offer?

6. At this point, you know that some of the guests did not give all the information about their accused murder. Who are they? What didn't they tell?

7. Who was the first Indian? How did he or she die? How did this relate to the rhyme?

8. How did the others explain the first death? Why was the explanation not really believable?

9. Irony is when things are not what they seem to be. What was ironic about the house?

10. What did Rogers notice? Why was that significant?

11. What common recollections did Wargrave, MacArthur, and Claythorne have at the end of Chapter 2?

Ten Little Indians
Chapters 6-8

Vocabulary

malicious   desultory   furtive   ruminating   chastisement
acquiesced   perpetrator   tabooed   proxy   incredulously
cavernous

1. What are the two titles of the book? What might they mean?

2. Who was the second to die? How did it happen? How did this relate to the poem?

3. What clues related to Dr. Armstrong?

4. What theories or speculations were voiced concerning why Mrs. Rogers died?

5. How was the General a pessimist?

6. How did Vera feel about Emily? Was she justified in feeling this way?

7. Armstrong and Lombard came to what conclusion? What did Lombard mean when he said, "There are crimes that cannot be brought home to their perpetrators"? Give two examples of such crimes.

8. What had Lombard, Armstrong, and Blore decided to do?

9. What was wrong with the General? How did this make Vera feel?

10. What conclusion did the three men reach about the murders? What is your opinion at this point?

11. At this point, which of the guests are suspected of being the murderer by the other guests? Do you think they are correct?

Ten Little Indians
Chapters 9-12

Vocabulary

perjury	noncommittal	succinctly	corroborate	idiosyncrasy
tenacious	acquitted	laconically	cumbrous	

1. What did Lombard realize about his mission to Indian Island?

2. What happened as the guests sat down to lunch?

3. What was Justice Wargrave's conclusion? What did the others think about it?

4. After the so-called trial, who do you think could be guilty?

5. Who did Lombard think the murderer was? Why?

6. Who did Vera believe was the murderer? Why?

7. How did the seven survivors guard against murder that night?

8. Who was the fourth Indian? How did he or she die?

9. What part did guilt play in this story? Identify and explain the guilt feelings of at least two characters.

10. How did the fifth Indian die?

11. What effects were the deaths having on the survivors and their relationships with one another?

12. List some clues and make a statement about who you think the murderer may be at this point in the story.

Ten Little Indians
Chapters 13–16

Vocabulary
sagacity   dogged   stealthy   conjuring   quietus
stolidly   abortive   lassitude   innocuous   solicitude
raucous

1. How were each of the five survivors acting and feeling? What tactics did they take to prevent another murder?

2. Describe what happened to Vera when she went to her room.

3. What happened to the judge?

4. Blore, Armstrong, and Lombard all thought they knew who the next victim would be. What guess would you make? Why?

5. What haunted Vera about Cyril's death? Do you think she was guilty of the murder? Explain.

6. Describe how Blore discovered that Armstrong was not in his room.

7. What is a red herring? What did Vera think it had to do with Armstrong's disappearance? How did she interpret the verse about the zoo?

8. What did Vera remember about the clock in her room? Which person (Vera, Armstrong or Lombard) do you think killed Blore? Why?

9. How did the two remaining Indians responded to one another? How would you act in a similar situation?

10. How did their relationship change when they found Armstrong? What happened next?

11. What happened at the end of Chapter 16? Why did the last Indian hang himself or herself?

Ten Little Indians
Epilogue and Manuscript

Vocabulary

sadistic	abhorrent	exigencies	incongruous
inexorable	maudlin	amoral	rendezvous	pagan
paradoxically			

1. Who was Morris? What was his connection to the mystery? Under what circumstances did he die?

2. What prompted the people on the mainland to investigate the island? What did the inspector feel had been the common motive for killing the ten people?

3. What was unusual about Vera's suicide? What did that imply?

4. How did the manuscript get to Scotland Yard?

5. What personal characteristics or fascinations did the author of the manuscript have that lead to his scheme?

6. What did the manuscript reveal about why the writer wanted to commit the murders and how he selected his victims?

7. Retell briefly how the murderer executed the demise of each of these people:

Tony	Mrs. R.	General
Rogers	Emily	Vera
Dr. A	Blore	Lombard
Judge Wargrave	Morris	

8. Why did the murderer decide to confess?

9. What three clues did the murderer think might have given him away?

10. Evaluate the judge's conclusion about his own guilt or deeds. Did he implement a perfect crime? Support your opinion.

Ten Little Indians
Conclusion and Summary

1. Agatha Christie's novels provide the reader with opportunities for mental gymnastics. Explain.

2. How is this book different from other mysteries?

3. What role did guilt play in the plot? Which murderer suffered the most from guilt? Which suffered the least? Why?

4. What techniques did Christie use to pull off this mystery? List at least three and explain each one.

5. What was Wargrave's motive for the murders? Do you agree or disagree with his reasoning?

6. The characters in this book had to face the challenge of staying alive but also had to deal with personal problems, conflicts, and personality flaws. Choose several characters and identify their internal conflicts.

7. At one point, Wargrave was accused of playing God. Was this true? Why or why not?

8. Would the mystery have been better without the epilogue and manuscript? Why?

9. Choose two characters in this story and compare and contrast their personalities, their crimes, and their reactions to events on the island.

10. Were there clues the people on the island overlooked that would have told them who the murderer was? If so, what were they?

Ten Little Indians

Activities

1. Plan and act out a mock trail for any one of the ten Indians. Choose classmates to be defendant, jury members, lawyers, and judge. Have the defendant and his/her lawyer draw upon Christie's characterizations for mannerisms and behavior.

2. Make a Ten Little Indians game that includes events and characters from this story.

3. Use another nursery rhyme and write an outline for your own mystery story using verses of the rhyme as clues.

4. Read another Christie mystery and summarize the book orally to the class. Be sure your synopsis does not give away the solution to the mystery. Compare the book to *Ten Little Indians*.

5. Design a program for the stage performance of *Ten Little Indians*. Include a synopsis, division according to acts, description of the characters and settings, and a cover illustration.

6. Write a script for a radio broadcast of one scene from this book. Tape your scene with special effects.

7. Make a map or model of the house and island showing where significant events occurred. Use details from the book as well as your imagination.

8. Write a series of three or four news articles that relate to events in this story that might have appeared in the Sticklehaven paper. Develop your own headlines and include important facts. Some possibilities might include Morris' obituary, the storm, Narracott's discovery of the bodies, Scotland Yard's investigation, or the discovery of Wargrave's letter.

9. Obtain a copy of the film version of *Ten Little Indians* or *And Then There were None*. Compare the book with the movie. Which was better? Why?

10. Recreate Vera Claythorne's diary. Include events as she saw them, her feelings about the happenings and other residents on the island, and her suspicions.

The Westing Game
Ellen Raskin

Suggested Reading Levels
Grades 6-8

Biography
Ellen Raskin was born on March 13, 1928. She was raised in Milwaukee, Wisconsin. As a child, she was surrounded by a large, extended family and experienced the Depression, which helped her develop a sense of humor as well as the work ethic. After majoring in art, she moved to New York, where she became a commercial illustrator and designer. She wrote and illustrated her first book for young readers in 1966. She married and had one child. Ellen earned the 1979 Newbery award for *The Westing Game*. Other titles include *Nothing Ever Happens on My Block*, *Figgs and Phantoms*, and *The Tattooed Potato and Other Clues*. She died in 1984.

Synopsis
Mystery

When Sam Westing's body is found, his sixteen nieces and nephews try to solve the puzzle surrounding his death. The rules and clues were arranged by Mr. Westing himself, and the winner becomes the heir to his fortune. The stakes are high and all the characters want to win. Among the candidates are young Turtle Wexler and her perfect and beautiful sister, Angela, Doug Hoo, high school track star, and Sandy McSouthers, the impoverished doorman of the Sunset Tower apartments, where, oddly all the characters reside. Humor and intrigue keep the readers spellbound from beginning to end.

Themes
1. Righteousness prevails
2. People depend on others
3. Guilt as a form of justice

Literary Objectives
1. Identify clues in a mystery
2. Utilize problem solving techniques
3. Analyze the elements of a mystery

Companion Titles
1. *Ten Little Indians* - Agatha Christie (elements of mystery, righteousness prevails, guilt as a form of justice)
2. *The Wolves of Willoughby Chase* - Joan Aiken (elements of mystery)

The Westing Game
Chapters 1–3

Vocabulary

grappled   gruesome   asylum   facade   podiatrist   gaunt
putrid

1. How does Ellen Raskin, the author, create suspense right away?

2. Identify some unusual circumstances found in Chapter One.

3. Who were the specially selected residents of the Sunset Towers? What varied occupations did they represent?

4. Describe the physical characteristics of each of the children in the Sunset Towers. Choose one adjective to describe each child's personality.

5. What happened to the two boys from Westingtown who went into the Westing estate on a dare?

6. Describe how Turtle and Angela were different? How did Mrs. Wexler treat them differently?

7. What was each person's response to Otis' claim that "Sam Westing was rotting away on an Oriental rug" at the Westing home?

8. What was wrong with Chris? What was his relationship with Theo?

9. What was Sydelle's outlook on life? Identify some of her suspicious or unusual behaviors.

The Westing Game
Chapters 4-7

Vocabulary

pyrotechnic	executor	trousseau	morbid	scrutiny
eccentric	purported	uncanny	pompous	jaunty	wafted

1. Why did Turtle go in the Westing house? What happened? What did she find?

2. Which facts in the newspaper article might be clues?

3. What things were not mentioned in the article?

4. Who was present for the reading of the will? Why did everyone have to go to the reading of the will?

5. Briefly describe each person's behavior upon arriving at the Westing library. What did these behaviors tell you about each character?

6. According to the will, what had happened to Samuel Westing?

7. What were some of the reactions to the first six clauses of the will?

8. What was the Westing Game? What were the rules?

9. What characters were on each team? How did they feel about their partners?

10. Explain several examples of humor in the book so far.

The Westing Game
Chapter 8

Vocabulary

buttressed   inscrutable   bigot   pretentious   hodgepodge
divisive   vindictiveness   impeccable

1. How did the snowstorm make the situation even more tense at Sunset Towers the next morning?

2. How did the author let you know Angela was sensitive? How did this change your mind about her character?

3. What did Turtle and Flora think their clues meant?

4. What was revealed about Grace's character?

5. What was the Sikes' connection with the murder?

6. How did Samuel Westing know the heir or heiress would play the game?

7. List all the clues given to each pair of players. What can you deduce from the clues?

8. Which pair seems to work together best? Worst? Why?

9. At this point in the book, several of the characters seemed more concerned with their problems or interests than in solving the mystery. Who were they and what were their concerns?

The Westing Game
Chapters 9–13

Vocabulary

humiliation   coiffure   pedicured   scornful   alibis
hysterical   paraphernalia   demeaning   elephantine

1. Why was Judge Ford giving a party?

2. At the beginning of Chapter 9 Grace Wexler's attitude toward Turtle changed for a short time. Why?

3. How did J.J. know Mrs. Wexler was pretending to be a relative of the Westings?

4. What were Angela and Sydelle trying to find out at the party?

5. What was Theo trying to find out?

6. What was accomplished at the coffee shop meeting?

7. What happened to end the meeting?

8. What did Turtle mean by "I don't need a crutch to get attention"? Did Turtle have a crutch? Explain.

9. Who were the four heirs with Westing connections? Explain the connections.

10. How were Angela's parents pressuring her into a life that was different from what she might choose for herself?

11. Was it a bomb or a gas explosion that exploded in the restaurant? Support and explain your answer with quotes.

The Westing Game
Chapters 14-20

Vocabulary

obsequious   soothsayer   incriminating   eluding   adjacent
penance   vagrancy   covetousness

1. What did Theo find out about the phrase, "May God thy gold refine"?

2. Why do you think Angela didn't expose Sydelle's deception? Why did she tell her she had an incurable disease? How was Angela changing?

3. What story did Sandy tell Turtle? Why did she think it was profound?

4. What information did Judge Ford obtain from the newspaper clippings and Sandy?

5. What did Sandy imply about Violet Westing?

6. What happened at the shower? Who did it? Why?

7. What were some of the solutions or clues offered in Chapter 17?

8. Why did Turtle buy more Westing stock? What were the results?

9. What new information was learned about Grace?

10. What did you learn about Sydelle?

11. What was George's connection to Westing?

12. What did Sandy and J. J. figure out?

The Westing Game
Chapters 21–30

Vocabulary

derelicts	meticulous	vengeful	unintelligible	derisive
paranoia	improbable	dastardly	stupefied	

1. What was Judge Ford's connection to Westing?

2. Who was the real bomber? Why did Turtle confess?

3. What did J. J. assume about Sam Westing?

4. What was missing from the song? Why was it significant?

5. What did the heirs conclude about Sandy? Why?

6. How was the Westing Game like chess?

7. What significant truths became known at the trial?

8. How did the heirs feel about playing the Westing Game?

9. What became of the Westing Estate?

10. What secret did T. R. keep?

11. The last chapter is entitled "The End?" Why is it a question?

The Westing Game
Conclusion and Summary

1. List at least three techniques Raskin used to make this a good mystery. Explain each technique.

2. In your opinion, what were Westing's motives?

3. How did the phrase "land of opportunity" figure into the theme of this mystery?

4. How did each of these characters change for the better? Explain what caused the changes in each of these characters:
   - Angela   -Sydelle
   - Turtle   -J.J. Ford

5. How was the game like life?

6. What role did guilt play in the mystery? Which characters felt guilty and why?

7. Many of the characters changed or benefitted from their association with their partners. Explain several of the positive relationships.

8. Explain how the mystery never ends. Explain how Sam Westing's inheritance continues to be re-invested.

9. How did each person benefit over the long run from participating in the Westing Game? Do you think they would have ended up the same if they had not played the game?

10. Do you think the game ended the way Sam Westing wanted? Explain.

11. Emotions were a part of this story and sometimes interfered with the characters' abilities to solve the mystery or cooperate. Give examples.

The Westing Game
Activities

1. Make a filmstrip, roller movie or video introducing *The Westing Game* to potential readers. Make one frame for each character and title and credit frames. Tell just enough to make your audience want to read the book themselves.

2. Design a real Westing Game. Make a game board and pawns. Write the objectives and directions for the game.

3. Read another book by Ellen Raskin and give an oral or written report on it. Include a paragraph that compares the book with *The Westing Game*.

4. Choose one of the sixteen heirs or heiresses to portray. Write a first-person monologue telling that person's function and point of view in the murder or the story. Include his or her personality, outlook on life, and opinion of the other players.

5. Research the game of chess. Give an oral or written report on the history of the game and compare it to the Westing Game.

6. Design a play program for the stage version of *The Westing Game*. Draw an intriguing cover giving credit to the author and scriptwriter. Divide the play into acts and inside the program include a synopsis of the setting for each act and list of characters as they appear.

7. Produce a radio broadcast of the most suspenseful scene from *The Westing Game*. Write out the script and develop your own sound effects.

8. Make a diorama or illustration of Turtle's closet bedroom, Westing's bedroom, the trial scene, or your favorite part of the mystery.

9. Create your own mystery that the heirs of T.R.'s inheritance will have to solve. Write an outline and brief description.

10. Choose at least five criterion to use to evaluate this book. Based on your rating, write a critical review, discussing the bad points, the good points, and why people your age might enjoy reading this book.